FIFTY WAYS TO PRACTICE SPEAKING

BELINDA YOUNG-DAVY

WAYZGOOSE PRESS

CONTENTS

INTRODUCTION

It takes many hours to become proficient at anything – a sport, a hobby, a musical instrument, or a foreign language. Many thousands of hours, in fact! For a student of English, this can seem difficult to accomplish, especially if your only opportunity to study English is in the classroom.

This book will help you practice speaking in English, both inside and outside the classroom. If you are already taking English classes, some of the tips will help you get more out of your classes. If you're not taking English classes – and even if you are – other tips will give you ideas to try on your own. Not every idea will work for every student. That's why there are fifty. We feel sure that many of the ideas presented here will bring you results if you try them sincerely.

Here is a suggested method for using this book:

1. Read through all of the fifty tips without stopping.
2. Read through the tips again. Choose five or six that

you think might work for you. Decide when you
will try them, and for how long.

3. Try to choose different types of ideas: some that
you can use in the classroom, some that you can use
on your own. You can choose some ideas that
require going online or using media, and some that
don't. Also, choose some that you can practice with
a friend or language learning partner, and some that
you can do alone.

4. Each time you use one of the ways, make a note
about how well it worked for you and why.
Remember that most of the tips will work best if
you practice them several times (or even make
them a habit). Don't try a tip only once and decide
it's no good for you. Give the tips you try a few
chances, at least.

5. Every few weeks, read through the ways again, and
choose some new ones. Discontinue using any
methods that are not working for you.

The most important advice, though, is to actually do the
suggestions you read about here. Wishing is not working. If
you don't do the work, you won't see the results.

❧ I ❦
IN CLASS OR WITH A
TEXTBOOK

MAKE ENGLISH A HABIT

It's important to use the English you already know as often as you can. Even repeating simple phrases will help with your pronunciation, intonation, and confidence.

For example, say *Hello, how are you?* and *Bye, see you on (Thursday)* to your teachers and classmates at every class. Of course you can just nod and wave, but then you are not practicing your speaking!

If you have a few minutes before class starts, make a general comment or ask a simple question. The best comments will be ones that encourage your classmates to respond to you— either to answer a question or share their own experience. Try something like one of these:

- *It's really cold today!*
- *Did you finish the homework yet?*
- *I'm really sleepy this morning.*
- *Do you have a (pencil/pen/piece of paper I could borrow?*
- *Are you going to the (game) this weekend?*

PRACTICE DIALOGUES

Most English textbooks contain short dialogues to listen to and practice. It's common for teacher to say, *Now practice the dialogue with a partner.*

When you practice a dialogue with a partner in class, make sure you both practice each role. Do each dialogue more than once. You will become more fluent every time you say it.

Check with your teacher to find out if there are other vocabulary words or different verb tenses that you can use in the dialogues, and make substitutions to create a new dialogue. Practice the new version several times too.

If there isn't time in class for enough practice, then practice at home with a classmate or friend. You can review dialogues from precious lessons, too.

❧ 3 ❧
SWITCH PARTNERS

When you practice a dialogue with a partner in class, change partners and do it again. Practice with as many different partners as you can.

It's good to get experience speaking with many different people. Everyone's voice sounds a little different, so you want to get used to hearing high voices and low voices, feminine voices and masculine voices, and of course different accents.

Watch your partners when you are speaking to them. Do they seem confused or frustrated? Maybe you need to slow down or to speak more clearly.

If your teacher doesn't give you opportunities to change partners in class, then sit in a different seat at every lesson. Most people tend to sit in the same place that they chose at the first class, so if you change seats, you will find new partners every lesson.

❧ 4 ❧

SPEAK WITHOUT READING.

When you and a partner are working with the textbook, practice the dialogue a few times. Then try saying it again but without looking at the book. We call this the "Look up and speak" technique.

If you forget what to say, quickly look down at the book, check the words, and then look up again.

If you are going to memorize a dialogue, this is a good inter-mediate step.

5

SAY IT OUT LOUD

Practice reading the dialogues (read both parts!) and the paragraphs in your textbook out loud at home.

You might feel foolish at first, but it's good practice. You can turn on the radio or some music to provide a little background noise, if that helps you feel more comfortable.

Just as in class, practice the texts more than once—in fact, until they feel easy to you. You can get creative and practice them in different voices—an old person, a child, someone angry, someone tired, someone excited, etc.

❧ 6 ❧

PLAN IN ADVANCE

Hopefully you are already using simple greetings and "small talk" with classmates. But you should also practice more advanced topics.

Before you come to class, plan a question to ask a classmate, or a piece of information that you want to say. Look up any vocabulary you need in advance. If you think your classmates won't know the new vocabulary, think of how you could easily explain it in English.

If time permits, ask your question or give your information to several people. Did they all respond in a similar way?

❧ 7 ❧

PRACTICE SYLLABLES

This technique will help your pronunciation especially of long or difficult words.

Practice the vocabulary lists in your textbook at home. Pronounce each syllable slowly two times; then say the word at normal speed the third time.

For example, to practice the word fundamentally, divide it into syllables:

- fun
- da
- ment
- al
- ly

So, practice (out loud!) *fun, fun, fun*, then *da, da, da*, then *ment, ment, ment*, and so on.

Then say the whole word. Pay attention to which syllable gets the most stress. In this case: *Fun-da-MENT-al-ly*.

Remember that many online dictionaries have spoken pronunciations of words that you can use to check yourself.

❧ 8 ❧

MEMORIZE A DIALOGUE

With a partner, choose a short dialogue in your textbook or a dialogue from an English story to completely memorize. Practice your part at home. Then every time you meet your partner, recite your dialogue.

Change to a new dialogue every month. Gradually increase the length of the dialogues.

Here are some resources for simple dialogues that are good to memorize:

An online collection of dialogues in different situations: https://www.eslfast.com/easydialogs/

Here is a full conversation textbook for beginners—free and legal to download as a .pdf—that also includes language notes for each dialogue: https://americanenglish.state.gov/resources/dialogs-everyday-use

There is also a similar book for intermediate and advanced students:
https://americanenglish.state.gov/resources/more-dialogs-everyday-use

And finally, here is a book with dialoguers for middle school and high school students (although obviously anybody could memorize them). The audio is available too.
https://americanenglish.state.gov/resources/everyday-conversations-learning-american-english

❧ 9 ☙

REVIEW REGULARLY

Every two or three weeks, practice dialogues or paragraphs from previous chapters in your textbook again. When you already understand the meaning completely, you can concentrate on pronunciation, intonation, and fluency.

If you have the dialogues on a CD or an mp3 file, say the sentences along with the speakers. This will help you work on your speed as well as your pronunciation. Try to imitate the speakers' accents. Remember to switch roles in the dialogues.

🦋 10 🦋

PRACTICE REACTING

Being a good speaker also means being a good listener.

React to good and bad news. Congratulate classmates in English when they answer a question correctly in class. Give classmates encouragement in English. Express sympathy or concern when classmates look tired or unhappy.

Here are some phrases you can use.

GOOD NEWS

- *That's great!*
- *That's wonderful!*
- *What good news!*
- *I'm really glad to hear that.*
- *Congratulations!* (Especially for getting married or engaged, winning a contest, getting hired or promoted art work)

BAD NEWS

I'm so sorry to hear that.

Sorry for your loss. (If someone the speaker knows, or their animal, has died.)

Let me know if I can do anything to help.

❧ II ❧
WITH A PARTNER OR GROUP OF FRIENDS

PRACTICE SPEAKING ON THE PHONE

Talking in a foreign language on the phone is especially difficult because you cannot see the other person's lips, expression, or body language—three things that normally help you understand someone else. In addition, when you are speaking, you cannot see from looking at the other person whether they are understanding you or not.

It's a good idea to practice speaking on the phone in a low-stress situation before you have to call about something important.

Call one of your classmates or an English-speaking friend on the phone and practice some of the dialogues in your textbook together. That way, you both know what to say, and what the other person said. Remember to practice both roles, and to repeat each dialogue a few times.

Of course, you can also practice free conversation—at the least, common greetings and small talk.

Learn some useful phrases to help you manage telephone conversations:

- *Sorry? Could you repeat that?*
- *Could you say that again?*
- *Could you explain that another way?*
- *Could you speak louder / more slowly / more clearly?*

If you don't have a local friend you can make a free call to, use an online app or program such as WhatsApp, Skype, or Facebook Messenger that will let you make free calls to most countries. Find another learner of English online (look on social media) and agree to become each other's speaking practice partner.

❧ 12 ❧

SHOW YOU ARE LISTENING

In every language, speakers use sounds to show that they are listening or to show that they're thinking about what to say next.

Listen for sentence fillers such as *um*, *uh*, *well*, and *you know* when you hear fluent speakers of English.

When you watch movies, television shows, talk shows, or interviews, pay attention to this kind of language. Notice how the sounds match the speaker's expressions and body language. In fact, sometimes it is useful to watch something in English and *only* listen for this kind of language—let the rest of the words go by.

When you speak English, make sure you make these sounds in English and not in your native language. This keeps your brain in English, and helps you speak more fluently.

13

MAKE A SPEAKING CIRCLE WITH FRIENDS

Exchange telephone numbers with two or three classmates. Call each classmate once a week and talk in English about one thing you did after class.

Talk for at least three minutes when you first start calling each other. Gradually increase the time to five minutes. If you keep your calls short, then people won't feel tired or pressured by this regular activity.

You can start by exchanging the same information with each person you call—you will notice it gets easier every time you practice. Then let the conversations develop naturally.

FIND A CONVERSATION PARTNER

Find a friend that you can meet with regularly for English conversation, perhaps while having coffee or tea or going for a walk.

Remember that it is just as useful to practice with someone who is also learning English as it is to practice with a fluent speaker. Sometimes, it is even easier, because you feel less pressure and can support each other.

If you don't already have a friend like this, advertise in local colleges and universities, at language schools, or on local message boards. Here is the sort of message you can post:

> Looking for an English conversation partner? I'm a university student, intermediate level in English, who wants to practice speaking English. We could meet at the university café on Wednesday or Friday afternoons. Text 555-5555 or email languagelearner@gmail.com.

You could also look for a language exchange, and speak for 15 minutes in English and 15 minutes in your native language, to help the person learning your language.

Just be careful meeting strangers—agree to meet the first few times in public places during the day. Tell a friend who you are meeting and when you will finish.

❧ 15 ❧

INTERVIEW A TEACHER IN
ENGLISH

You can ask to meet with a teacher who speaks English even if you are not taking a class with that teacher.

Make sure you know what you want to talk about before you go. For example, you could ask three to five questions asking for advice on how to improve your English. You could ask about jobs in your field that involve speaking English. You could talk about a special interest or hobby of that teacher, if you know they have one.

Remember to make an appointment in advance, so the teacher will have time to talk to you.

❧ 16 ❧

GET INVOLVED

Whaat do you like to do? What are your hobbies and interests? Do you play sports, play a musical instrument, make things, paint or draw, dance, spend time with animals, play board games ... ?

Find a group that does what you enjoy, and join them. Of course, if you join such a group in an English-speaking country, you will have opportunities to speak in English with other members.

But if you don't, look for an international group of people... or create one yourself! You can advertise that it is meant for people of all nationalities, and that the common language will be English.

This is a great way to learn specialized vocabulary for something you enjoy doing.

❧ 17 ❧

PRACTICE SERVICE ENCOUNTERS

If you are in an English-speaking country, every time you go to the store, greet the store clerk in English and make a comment or ask a question:

- *Hello, how are you today?*
- *The weather is very nice today, isn't it? Isn't it cold!*
- *Do you have any fresh flowers today?*
- *Can you recommend a local wine?*

Of course, if the store is busy, keep your conversations brief, and don't keep talking if the other person looks busy.

You can also ask people on the street to give you directions to some place nearby. Be sure to thank them for their time.

CALL BUSINESSES

If you are in an English-speaking country, you can practice English by calling different businesses and asking for information. For example, call a store and ask about opening and closing times or other information.

You can also call places in a non-English speaking country that probably have English speakers, such as international airlines and embassies or consulates.

Note that larger businesses might not have a person answering the phone, and instead use recorded messages. That won't help you with speaking practice, although it is useful listening practice!

PLAY A GUESSING GAME

Play *Who Am I? / What is it?* with friends.

Each of you will be famous person or an object. Other players have to guess who or what you are. Take turns asking questions to guess the person's identity. For example:

- *Are you a person?*
- *Are you a musician?*
- *Do you live in this country or in a foreign country?*
- *Do you have short hair?*
- *Are you made of metal?*
- *Are you smaller than a car?*

Variation: To make the game a little more difficult, limit the group to only 20 questions.

PLAY ENGLISH WORD GAMES WITH CLASSMATES

Here are some word games to play in English:

The Alphabet Game. One person says a letter of the alphabet, such as E. Other players take turns saying words that begin with E (*egg, elephant, easy*) and a sentence using that word (*I like eggs, I've never seen an elephant, Speaking English is easy*).

The Chain Game. Sit in a circle. One person says a sentence like this: *I went shopping and bought (an apple)*. The next person repeats that sentence and adds another word: *I went shopping and I bought an apple and (a banana)*. Continue around the circle. You can choose words in alphabetical order or just any words. See how long you can keep going before someone forgets something!

The Geography Game. One person says the name of a capital city or country (if you like, you can add states and provinces). The next person has to say another place that begins with the last letter of the previous word. For example:

- Spai**n**
- **N**ew Zealan**d**
- **D**enmar**k**
- **K**eny**a**
- **A**then**s**

and so on. Play stops when someone cannot think of a place. (You will find that you need many places that begin with A!)

Remember to use the English versions of place names—for example, the capital of Austria is Vienna, and not Wien (as it is in German).

This is a good way to practice your geography as well as your English!

GHOST. One person starts by saying a single letter. The next person says a letter that is part of a word, and so on around the circle. Each person must be thinking of a real word, but it doesn't have to be the same word. The goal is to keep going as long as possible without finishing a word. If someone finishes a word or cannot continue without finishing a word, they lose. Each time someone loses, they get a letter from the word "GHOST"—when they have all five letters, they lose the game.

Here is an example of the game played by four people:

A: e (thinking of "exit")
B: ex (thinking of "extra")
C: exp (thinking of "explain")
D: expo (thinking of "exposition"

A: expon (thinking of "exponent")
B: exponen (thinking of "exponent)
C: exponent (thinking of "exponentially")

Player C loses this round, because even though they were thinking of "exponentially," they finished the word "exponent," which is a complete word. Therefore, they earn the letter G.

❧ III ❧
BY YOURSELF

READ A PARAGRAPH ALOUD

It's useful to practice monologues as well as dialogues and conversations.

Choose a paragraph from your textbook, a novel, an article, whatever you like. Read it aloud. Start with a short one at first, and then as you repeat this exercise, you can use longer ones.

The first time you read it, you will probably be concentrating on meaning. So, read it again – several times – and also concentrate on thought groups, tone of voice, and punctuation. Remember to pause a little when you see a comma, and a little longer when you see a period.

❧ 22 ❧

SHADOW

Find a short clip on YouTube such as a scene from a TV show, a commercial, or a short talk. Look for one with closed captioning (subtitles in English), marked with CC at the bottom of the screen.

Listen to your piece a few times. Play it both with and without the captions. Look up any vocabulary you don't know.

Then turn on the captions and read along. Try to match the pronunciation and also the speed. Keep practicing! This is called "shadowing." Eventually, see if you can turn off the captions and just speak along with with the show without reading.

❧ 23 ❧

RECORD ON YOUR PHONE

Record new vocabulary words or phrases on your cell phone. Then practice using the words/phrases in three or four sentences right away at home by yourself.

This will make it easier to use the vocabulary with other people in the future. If you are in an English-speaking country, try use the vocabulary naturally in conversation at least two times in the same week that you learn it. Remember the phrase, "Use it or lose it!"

You can combine this tip with other tips such as #11 (Practice speaking the phone) or #13 (Make a speaking circle).

⚜ 24 ⚜

MAKE VOCABULARY CARDS

Write a definition and the pronunciation of five to ten words each week. Write two sentences for each word. For example, copy one sentence from the dictionary, and write one sentence of your own.

Carry the cards with you so that you can practice saying the sentences whenever you have some free time (and some privacy!).

One convenient way to carry cards is to punch a hole in one corner and then put them all on a metal ring.

❧ 25 ❧

USE LABELS

Label objects in one or more rooms in your house with tape and a marker. Say the name of an object at least three times every day (like when you enter the room) for one or two weeks.

If you like (and if you live alone), you can even have short conversations with your objects: *Hello, Ms. Refrigerator! How are you? I'd like you to meet Mr. Rice Cooker.*

Later, practice describing objects in the rooms to friends to classmates.

❧ 26 ❧

RECORD AN ENGLISH PHONE
MESSAGE

Record an answering machine message for your phone in English. (If this would confuse people who regularly call you, then make a bilingual message.)

You might want to write out your message first and practice it several times first.

Change your message every few weeks.

✣ 27 ✣

KEEP A SPEAKING DIARY

We usually think of a diary or journal as a written account, but you can also make one by speaking.

Keep an oral diary by recording your thoughts or ideas about a topic, or by talking about what you did that day. Say seven to ten sentences each time. If you have trouble saying ten sentences about what you did, you can also talk about what you did *not* do.

Make a diary entry at least three times a week. Put it on your calendar so you don't forget.

After a few months, go back and listen to some of your earlier entries. See how much you have improved!

❧ 28 ❧

DESCRIBE THINGS YOU KNOW

One thing you can talk about is something you know well.

Describe a different room in your house every day (at least five sentences): for example, what objects are there? Where are they? What colors are the wall, curtains, the carpet? Is it a light room or a dark room?

You can also describe places outdoors or buildings you know.

Look up any new vocabulary that you need for the descriptions; you might want to review prepositions of place. Practice describing rooms to friends and classmates.

❧ 29 ❧

RESEARCH A TOPIC

Choose a topic—it can be a hobby or special interest, but you could also choose to learn about a new topic.

Go online or read in a magazine or book to find five new words or expressions related to that topic. Practice saying sentences with them out loud by yourself, if possible; then say those sentences to another language learner or an English-speaking friend.

Every week, learn a few more words and expressions. Soon you will be able to speak easily about that topic!

❦ 30 ❦

TELL JOKES

Learn and practice a joke in English. When you have memorized the joke, tell it to as many people as you can!

You can find lists of jokes in English online. You can look for general jokes or specific types. Here are some useful sites:

GENERAL

https://english-at-home.com/funny-jokes/

This site also explains the jokes.

KNOCK-KNOCK JOKES

These depend on another person to take the B part and respond in the correct way. Most English-speaking people will know this pattern. The last line involves a pun. For example:

A: Knock, knock!
B: Who's there?
A: Olive.
B: Olive who?
A: Olive you! (= *I love you*)

https://bestlifeonline.com/knock-knock-jokes/

DAD JOKES

This is a term for jokes that usually involve puns or some kind of word play. They are not about fathers, but Americans often say that fathers tell this kind of joke.

https://www.fatherly.com/life/dad-jokes

❧ 31 ❧

KEEP A TRAVEL PLAN DIARY

Where do you dream of going? What do you want to do and see there?

Every week (or several times a week), look up two facts about a country or city that you want to visit and record them.

If you need to know how to pronounce cities, landmarks, or special places in your country, you can often find the correct pronunciation on YouTube by searching for (for example) "pronounce Edinburgh."

Eventually, you can use the information you learned to write and record a short presentation about the place.

🎔 32 🎔

SLOWLY INCREASE SPEAKING
PRACTICE

It's good to practice reading a long passage out loud (see tip #21), but it's also good to practice speaking for a longer time without reading.

Find a picture in a magazine and record a short story about it. Speak for two minutes.

The next time you practice, add another 30-60 seconds. Continue until you build up to five minutes.

Here are some sentences to get you started:

Once upon a time, there lived a ...

❈ 33 ❈

PRACTICE THINKING IN ENGLISH

Pick a topic. Give yourself one minute to think about it, and then record yourself talking about the topic for two minutes.

Do this every week, but reduce the thinking time by fifteen seconds and the speaking time by thirty seconds every week until you reach thirty seconds for thinking and sixty seconds for speaking.

Note: This is very good practice for the speaking section on the TOEFL iBT exam, which has very short preparation times and speaking times.

❦ IV ❦
PRONUNCIATION

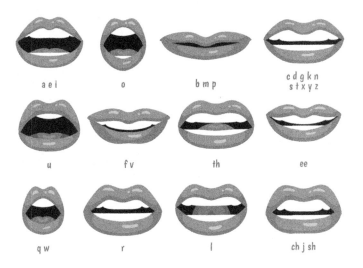

❧ 34 ❧

SPEAK LOUDLY

It's natural for some learners of another language to speak softly—they're nervous about making mistakes, or perhaps they feel embarrassed about their pronunciation.

However, your pronunciation improves when you speak loudly, and so does your confidence. You don't have to yell, but be aware of your own volume and do your best to speak as loudly as you can without seeming strange.

If you find this difficult, practice speaking out loud when you are alone at home. Put on some music without lyrics, or perhaps put on the radio or television loudly enough to make a little noise but softly enough that you can't make out the words. Then when you talk, speak loudly enough to cover the background noise.

Singing along with the radio or an album is another way good way to work on your volume.

❧ 35 ❧

USE THOUGHT GROUPS

Do not say each word in a sentence separately. Speak in "thought groups" – for example, subject + verb (*He's running*) or a prepositional phrase (*to the beach*). Practice linking the end of one word to the beginning of another. Listen to native or fluent English speakers to see how they do this.

For example, a sentence like

I'm thinking about going to a concert with my friend Amy

would be divided into thought groups like this:

> *I'm thinking about*
> *going to a concert*
> *with my friend Amy*

Remember that the end consonant of one word will join with the vowel sound of the next word (*friend Amy* = *fren damy*).

However, when one word ends with an "oo" sound or an "oh" sound and joins to a word starting with a vowel, you add a "w" sound: *to a = toowa*.

When a word ends with an "ee" or "eye" sound and the next word begins with a vowel, join them by adding a "y" sound: *the arm = thee yarm*.

USE AN ONLINE DICTIONARY

Find and use an online English-English dictionary to improve your pronunciation. Most online dictionaries have a pronunciation feature. Type in the word you want to practice. Listen to the pronunciation at least four times before you try to pronounce it.

Pronounce the word more slowly than the native speaker at first. Pay attention to the number of syllables in the word and which syllable has a stress mark. Notice how the vowel in stressed syllables is pronounced longer, higher (in pitch), and a little louder.

TRY DIFFERENT PRONUNCIATION
STYLES

Practice reading a dialogue with different voices—this could be different accents (for example, American, British, Australian) or different feelings (sad, bored, excited).

To hear different accents, listen to examples on YouTube. You can search by searching, for instance, for "Scottish accent" or "Australian accent." Compare different native English accents, such as English, Irish, Scottish, American, Canadian, South African, Indian, Australian, New Zealander. (Of course, there are several varieties of accent inside these countries too.)

It's also a good idea to listen to non-native speaker accents —after all, there are more non-native speakers of English in the world than there are native speakers! Search for accents you are likely to hear—those from countries near you or that you might visit or do business with.

❧ 38 ❧

PRACTICE SPEAKING IN FRONT OF
A MIRROR

Are you making facial expressions that show your feelings? If you have trouble pronouncing some sounds in English, check some videos on YouTube and similar sites that demonstrate mouth positions for those sounds.

To speak English clearly, you may have to practice opening your mouth wider when you say words. Check yourself in the mirror often.

You can also videotape yourself speaking, and watch the video later to see how you are doing.

❧ 39 ❧

BECOME AN ACTOR

Practice reading and reciting the dialogues with emotion. Exaggerate! Use a lot of word stress and intonation. Sometimes it helps to pretend you are a different person a different kind of person.

Remember to pause for a moment when you see a comma (,) and a little longer at the end of sentences.

You may feel foolish because many languages do not emphasize sounds in the same way that English does. But often the point at which you feel you are overdoing the intonation is the point at which you actually sound like a native speaker.

❧ 40 ❧

PAY ATTENTION INTONATION AND WORD STRESS

Have you ever experienced walking though an international airport or train station, and you knew someone was speaking your language, even though you couldn't make out any words? How did you know it was your language? You could tell by the intonation—the "music" of the sentence.

Do not worry too much about pronouncing specific letters or sounds such as *l*, *th*, *v*, etc.

Instead, focus on intonation, word stress, and expression. A single sound made incorrectly will almost never make it difficult for someone to understand you. However, unnatural intonation is very difficult for native speakers to follow.

Remember too that it is better to speak more slowly and clearly than to try to sound fluent by speaking too fast.

GET CREATIVE

✌ 41 ✌

PRACTICE WITH THE TELEVISION

Remember tip #23, Shadow? Shadowing is a great technique to use with TV shows and movie clips.

If you are in an English-speaking country, use local TV's closed captioning (CC) while watching English programs. You can also use a TV show on a streaming service such as Netflix, Hulu, Disney+, and so on. Almost all of their offerings will have a way to turn on English captions, or even English subtitles to translated shows.

Turn off the sound and turn on the closed captioning. Choose one of the characters and say the character's lines while you are watching the program. You might find it a challenge at first, because it will go fast—but repeated practice will help you speak (and read!) more quickly.

❧ 42 ❧

LEARN A SONG

Songs are a wonderful way to practice speaking because you can find ones that are slow and yet still have natural connections between words. And, of course, they are enjoyable!

Choose a song, look up the lyrics online, and then practice singing along with a performance on YouTube.

It doesn't matter what song you learn—you can learn your favorite pop song, a song for children, a traditional folk song... why not learn several types of songs? You might find folk songs easy to understand and sing because they are typically slow. Children's songs often have a lot of repetition, which makes them easy. But the best kind of song is a song that you genuinely like.

Note that some internet sites have incorrect lyrics to songs, so it's good to check in more than one place, just to be sure. This is also true of songs on YouTube to which fans have added the lyrics as subtitles. However, one or two spelling mistakes in YouTube lyrics won't hurt you or your progress in English.

If you really like a song, buy it and put it on your phone or mp3 player!

If you have karaoke bars in your city, practice some English songs that you can sing when you go out. You could even challenge some friends to go out for karaoke and only sing in English!

❦ 43 ❧

CREATE A TIKTOK

Watch some examples of TikToks or reels on Instagram. Which ones do you like? Why?

Plan one of your own! Decide what you will say, practice a few times, and then record yourself and post it.

Here are a few ideas:

- A food from my country
- How to (do something)
- Why I love (something)
- My pet
- A tour of my room
- Something I'm proud of
- Something I do well

You can always delete your post later if you don't like it. However, it's a good idea to not worry too much about being perfect. Just be human!

❧ 44 ❧

CREATE A ROLE PLAY WITH
FRIENDS

With a group of friends, write a role play (or find one in a textbook). Have everyone practice their part for a week. If possible, have a few rehearsals together. Remember to use emotion and to exaggerate your intonation when you are saying your part.

When everybody feels ready, record the role play with your cell phone. Watch your video together. Decide where you can improve your pronunciation or intonation. Practice again and then make a new video. Compare the videos to see how you improved.

❧ 45 ❧

WRITE AN ORIGINAL SONG

Write and sing a simple song in English that uses phrases and words you already know.

For a great example of this, watch on YouTube the *One Semester of Spanish Spanish Love Song*. This is a "love song" made up of only the phrases and sentences the singer learned during one semester of Spanish study—including phrases such as *Happy birthday*, *I like the library*, *I have two bicycles*, and *I live in a red house*.

This link worked in 2023, but if it doesn't work for you, just search for the title on YouTube:

https://www.youtube.com/watch?v=ngRq82c8Baw

If you don't think you can write an original tune, or if you don't want to, then use a tune you already know, and write new lyrics.

❧ 46 ☙

HAVE A FASHION SHOW

Do you love clothes, colors, and patterns? Dress up and have a fashion show with friends at someone's house!

Each person will take a turn as the announcer and describe someone's hairstyle, clothes, and accessories. Research vocabulary about clothing, fabrics, and patterns. Use at least three sentences to describe each person.

If you like, video the performance and decide if you would do anything differently next time.

❧ 47 ❧

PRACTICE WITH A MOVIE

Watch a DVD of an English movie you have already seen. Pick a scene in the movie that you liked. Choose one of the characters in one scene and repeat everything the character says. Then turn off the sound and say your character's lines. If you say them a little differently, that is fine! You don't have to memorize the character's lines for this technique to work well.

Do this several times in one month, choosing a different scene every time.

✢ 48 ✢

CREATE AN ENGLISH SKIT

Work with a group of friends and create a short skit.

For a good example, watch *Que Hora Es?* on YouTube. The actors in this "soap opera" are beginning Spanish students, and all of the sentences come from the first three weeks of a Spanish class—such as *What time is it? It's eight o'clock.* However, the sentences are said in a dramatic way, to communicate a different meaning, such as *Who are you? What are you doing?*

Here is a link that worked in 2023, but if it doesn't work for you, just search for the title. (There's a Part 2, too!)

https://www.youtube.com/watch?v=4cKGyOE_jOI

With your group, think of a situation. Then use the sentences in your previous lessons to make the "script." Act out your script. If possible, record it and show it to your class.

❧ 49 ❦
RAP IT

Rap is a wonderful way to practice English because you can really "play" with the language. You don't need exact rhymes or a strict structure.

Write an English rap song about your hobby, school, job, or current events. Perform it for friends.

❧ 50 ❧

MEMORIZE A POEM

Recite it for friends, classmates, or teachers. In English, try to explain why you chose the poem and what it means.

Here is an example of a short poem:

A Very Short Song (Dorothy Parker)

Once, when I was young and true,
Someone left me sad –
Broke my brittle heart in two;
And that is very bad.

Love is for unlucky folk,
Love is but a curse.
Once there was a heart I broke;
And that, I think, is worse.

Here are some sites where you can find poems:

https://hackspirit.com/25-beautiful-short-poems-that-will-tug-at-your-heart-strings/

https://www.weareteachers.com/24-must-share-poems-for-middle-school-and-high-school/

Some poems in English have aa special rhythm. A **limerick** is one of these. Listen to some examples of this kind of five-line poem on YouTube until you know the rhythm.

> I'd rather have fingers than toes;
> I'd rather have ears than a nose.
> And as for my hair,
> I'm glad it's all there;
> I'll be awfully sad when it goes.

Here are two sites with some limericks:

https://parade.com/1249429/marynliles/limericks/

https://www.rd.com/list/limericks-for-kids/

If a poem seems too long, you can do the same activity with a quotation. Search online for quotations about a certain topic (such as *famous quotation + friendship*).

BONUS TIP!

SOCIALIZE AND SPEAK

Research has shown that drinking a moderate amount of alcohol can improve your speaking ability—because you are more relaxed and not afraid of making mistakes and taking chances.

Invite some friends to a bar (choose a quiet one where you can hear each other speaking, of course!) or host a cocktail hour at someone's house.

Of course, too much alcohol consumption makes speaking English (and even your native language) more difficult. Be a responsible language learner!

OTHER BOOKS IN THE SERIES

Of course, no one skill in English is really separate from the others. Speaking, listening, reading, and writing are all connected. Improving in one area will almost always bring improvements to other areas too.

Consider trying some of the other books in our *Fifty Ways to Practice* series. As of 2023, we have guides for

- Listening
- Speaking
- Reading
- Writing
- Grammar
- Vocabulary
- Business English

Is there something else you would like to practice? Send an email to editor@wayzgoosepress.com and let us know!

AFTERWORD

Learning another language is never fast, but the *Fifty Ways to Practice* series will speed things up by showing you how to practice more efficiently and effectively, both inside and outside the classroom. It is useful for beginning through advanced levels. The *Fifty Ways to Practice* series offers short, practical guides to different areas of English language study for motivated students.

Note: We have priced these *Fifty Ways to Practice* guides very cheaply, because we want education and learning to be available to as many people as possible. However, our authors are highly qualified professionals who work hard to create these books. If these books are useful to you, please recommend them to your friends—but please do not share them freely. Our authors will continue to write excellent and cheap books for you if they make a little money. That way, we all win. Thank you for your support!

If you have comments or suggestions (such as ideas for future books that you would find useful), feel free to contact the publisher at editor@wayzgoosepress.com, check out the offerings on our publishing website at http://wayzgoosepress.com or join us on Facebook.

To be notified about the release of new 50 Ways titles, as well as other new titles and special contests, events, and sales from Wayzgoose Press, please sign up for our mailing list. (We send email infrequently, and you can unsubscribe at any time.)

Made in the USA
Las Vegas, NV
03 October 2024